Women's Guide to Divorce in Florida

Heather B. Quick, Esquire
The Quick Law Group

Call The Quick Law Group at 904-241-0012 for a consultation about your Florida divorce, or to learn more please visit TheQuickLawGroup.com.

Table of Contents

Title Page..1

Table of Contents...2

Introduction...3

What Happens During a Florida Divorce – a General Overview.......................4

Florida Divorce Process: the Critical Basics...6

Time Sharing: Child Visitation and Custody in Florida...................................8

Domestic Violence: What You Need to Know...10

Alimony in Florida: Important Terms and Ideas..12

Division of Marital Property and Assets..14

Litigation vs. Mediation..16

Child Support in Florida: Key Terms and Ideas...18

FAQs About Divorce in Florida..20

Using the "5 Whys" to Understand the Roots of Your Divorce-Related Problems............24

Feel More Energized and Healthy By Improving Your Diet..............................26

Get Calmer and Reduce Anxiety by Practicing Mindfulness.............................28

Obtaining Social Support..30

Journaling..32

Get Organized and Clearheaded...34

Interview with Heather Quick..36

Conclusion...42

Disclaimer...43

Call The Quick Law Group at 904-241-0012 for a consultation about your Florida divorce, or to learn more please visit TheQuickLawGroup.com.

Introduction

Perhaps your husband left you out of the blue, after a fight at the dinner table. Or maybe, after months of therapy, you've come to the painful realization that your marriage just can't work.

In either case, you're probably feeling overwhelmed, confused and scared about how your life is changing. This guide can help. It offers practical tips to make the divorce process simpler and more likely to lead to a positive outcome. It also serves as a reference guide, so if/when you have questions about the divorce process -- which is all but inevitable -- you can use it to troubleshoot issues and regain equilibrium and clarity.

The book is broken into three main sections:

In Part One, we'll review Florida's divorce process, so you know exactly what's coming and what the important terms are. You'll also learn about best practices and common mistakes women make during divorce. Finally, an "FAQ" answers key questions many clients have.

Part Two introduces you to useful tools and resources to help you structure your life, get organized, get relaxed, plan financially and rebuild your life and social network after the divorce.

Part Three features an interview with me, during which I discuss my passion for helping women like you through divorce. You will learn how my process typically works and what distinguishes my approach from the way other Florida divorce attorneys work.

The Goal of This Book: More Clarity and More Ease

This guidebook aims to empower you during your Florida divorce. You'll learn strategies for how to feel less overwhelmed, how to communicate your needs and how to transform this experience into something, if not outright "positive," then at least useful and instructive.

Note: This is not a "Do it Yourself" divorce book: the legal process is quite complicated and technical. The insights here should not serve as a substitute for guidance from an attorney. Rather, the book provides an overview of key concepts that you should know and practice.

A third of all people who marry ultimately get divorced. But most women never imagine that "it could happen to me." Even if you have friends and family standing by you, here's the cold reality: *it often gets worse before it gets better.* That might sound like bad news, since you may already feel pretty lousy.

On the other hand, there is good news. *Over the long term, you WILL bounce back.* And if you
Call The Quick Law Group at 904-241-0012 for a consultation about your Florida divorce, or to learn more please visit TheQuickLawGroup.com.

approach the divorce strategically -- and treat yourself with compassion and kindness -- you can emerge from this experience stronger, more resilient, more optimistic and happier.

Thank you again for trusting me to serve as your guide… and let's get to the tips!

What Happens During a Florida Divorce – a General Overview

Every divorce is different, in much the same way that every relationship is different. But common themes emerge in most cases. What are they? What are the typical "big issues" that divorcing women face, and how should you approach them?

Florida Statute 61.031 defines divorce as a "dissolution of marriage." Whether you were married for six months or 60 years, you may need to confront these challenges:

Dividing up the marital estate and assets.

How much money, property, and other assets have you and your husband accumulated? What is your current financial situation, and what are your financial end goals?

If your finances are disorganized -- or if you've been kept in the dark about them -- do not panic. However, to protect yourself (and your assets), you will likely want to conduct a thorough inventory, so you and your attorney know exactly what's at stake.

Alimony.

Will your husband have to pay you alimony? If so: how much, how frequently, and under what conditions? (Alternatively, will you have to pay your husband alimony? If so: how much, how frequently, and under what conditions?)

Alimony is a regular stipend that one spouse collects to pay for critical essentials, like living expenses, clothing and food. The alimony amount can be modified over time. For instance, perhaps 2 years from now, you'll get a new job or receive a big promotion, or your needs will increase. In that case, the alimony will need to be changed.

Child support, visitation, and custody.

Who will make critical decisions about the welfare, healthcare, religious upbringing and education of your children from the marriage? How will visitation and custody arrangements work? Will you (or your husband) have to pay child support? How and when can such arrangements be amended, and how can you protect yourself and your child?

Call The Quick Law Group at 904-241-0012 for a consultation about your Florida divorce, or to learn more please visit <u>TheQuickLawGroup.com</u>.

Florida law distinguishes between **"legal custody"** (i.e. who gets to make decisions about the child's healthcare, schooling, etc.) and **"physical custody"** (i.e. who gets to spend time with the child and under what circumstances).

We'll cover all these concepts and address key nuances about them soon. For now, appreciate the following key takeaways:

- **The divorce process can take a fair amount of time.** The glacial pace can be agonizing, but you need to be patient and engage with the process effectively.

- **Every divorce is unique.** To the extent you can, avoid comparing your divorce to other people's divorces, not only to protect your sanity but also to ensure that you find a strategy that works for your needs and values.

- **Litigation may be necessary, and the process should not be feared, if you have an attorney who understands it well.** Sometimes, parties can resolve negotiations over assets, alimony, child custody, and child support outside the courtroom. But you may need to go to court to fight vigorously to get what you want and what your family needs.

Call The Quick Law Group at 904-241-0012 for a consultation about your Florida divorce, or to learn more please visit TheQuickLawGroup.com.

Florida Divorce Process: the Critical Basics

Every case differs, but this outline follows how most Florida divorces unfold. By understanding this process, you'll be better prepared to achieve a fair resolution.

How the Florida divorce process works

Phase I

- **Qualifying.** Florida requires six months' residency in the state, but no waiting period before filing for divorce. After filing, a couple must wait 20 days before finalizing the divorce.

- **Initiating.** Either the husband or wife files a dissolution of marriage, either in the county where the couple last resided together or where the other spouse lives now. The filing spouse may also file for alimony or child support through the family department of the county circuit court.

- **Within 20 days, the husband must answer.** If desired, the husband may file his own petition to challenge any issues mentioned in the wife's petition.

Phase II

- **Next comes the "discovery process,"** which includes the husband and wife submitting financial affidavits detailing their assets and debts. Discovery rules protect you from hidden assets.

- **The case will go to mediation, as the law requires mediation.**

Phase III

- **Trial, if negotiations don't succeed.** If the couple fails to arrive at a mutually satisfying agreement, the case may go to trial (litigation). If the divorce goes to court, attorneys for each spouse work out issues such as child responsibility, alimony, visitation, and dividing debt and assets. A judge must determine the outcome.

Call The Quick Law Group at 904-241-0012 for a consultation about your Florida divorce, or to learn more please visit TheQuickLawGroup.com.

Mistakes Women Make in the Divorce Process

- **Disorganization.** Mislaying papers may cause costly mistakes. Sort and file paperwork chronologically or into categories that make sense to you.

- **Confidentiality.** Keep everything from your attorney in a safe place.

- **Allowing emotions to drive decisions.** Focus on what helps you rebuild your life.

- **Leaving all the legwork to your attorney.** Especially if you're on a budget (time or financial), do all you can to help your attorney by submitting paperwork quickly. Scan and email paperwork or drop it off, for example, instead of postal mailing it.

- **Forgetting how divorce impacts children.** Spend extra time with your children and listen to their questions. It's okay if you don't have all the answers. Be empathetic.

- **Neglecting self-care.** Continue to do activities that help you de-stress, such as exercise, reading or hobbies. Eat right and get enough rest. Let go of negative emotions that tear you apart. Surround yourself with positive people and influences.

Summary

The steps in a divorce may take unexpected detours, but staying true to what's important to you will help you arrive at the destination you want.

Call The Quick Law Group at 904-241-0012 for a consultation about your Florida divorce, or to learn more please visit TheQuickLawGroup.com.

Time Sharing: Child Visitation and Custody in Florida

Parents shape their children's lives immeasurably. Children better understand and accept their parents' divorce if their parents work together as civilly as possible. The biggest factors in divorces involving children include **who receives custody** (the home where the children will live) and **visitation** (scheduled visits with the children for the non-custodial spouse).

Parental Responsibility

Florida courts' use of "parental responsibility," not "custody," underscores the importance of both parents. It also lessens the thought of children as "assets" to win. Understand: the measuring tool is "best interests of the children," not "what my husband wants."

Important Terms

- **"Sole parental responsibility"** (formerly "sole custody"): the child resides exclusively with one parent, who makes all decisions regarding the children's care. This is an extreme measure for situations where "sharing" could be harmful.

- **"Shared parental responsibility"** (formerly "joint custody"): both parents help make decisions on the children's behalf.

- **"Time sharing schedule"** The parents and court formulate the time sharing schedule, which determines when the children spend time with each parent.

- **"Supervised visitation"** children must be supervised when they visit with the parent who is not given non-sole parental responsibility. This usually occurs in abuse cases and may or may not be temporary.

Mistakes Women Make During the Process of Determining Parental Responsibility

- **Representing yourself.** Even if your spouse completely cooperates with your wishes, you generally want an attorney to keep agreements legally binding.

- **Procrastinating.** Submitting paperwork and information on time shows your responsible character to the court.

- **Trying to deny visitation.** Unless your husband has abused the children or threatens violence, don't try to deny visitation. Doing so makes you appear vengeful at best and dishonest at worst.

Call The Quick Law Group at 904-241-0012 for a consultation about your Florida divorce, or to learn more please visit TheQuickLawGroup.com.

- **Dredging up unrelated information.** Focus on the parent/child relationship, not on the spousal relationship.

- **Cohabiting.** The court may look upon your situation unfavorably, if a new love interest moves in or sleeps over during the process.

- **Exhibiting anger/depression.** Keep your cool, and focus on the positives to maintain your status as a competent, poised and capable parent.

- **Leaving your home.** The court usually favors keeping children in their home. Unless your husband is abusive, leaving can make you appear unstable. It's better to have him legally removed, if necessary, for safety.

- **Remaining unemployed.** Even if you don't have your dream job, staying employed shows that you have the intention and ability to provide for the children.

Best Practices for Visitation and Parental Responsibility

Let's say that Kayla, a 31-year-old, separated from Ed, her husband of seven years. He had a quiet affair with the teacher of their daughter, Anna, 6. Now Kayla cannot stand the sight of Michelle, the teacher. The court granted Ed visitation with their daughter. Kayla knows better than to bad-mouth Ed to her: Anna can't keep secrets. But Kayla pulls Anna from her school and enrolls her in a school inconveniently located to Ed's workplace. He must drive 45 minutes out of his way to pick her up. As sole contact with the new school, Kayla can keep Ed jumping by sharing information at the last minute. It may appear Kayla gained the upper hand, but manipulating circumstances to get revenge always looks bad. Kayla has also disrupted Anna's life in yet another way, which makes her appear unstable. Since Anna doesn't know of Ed's infidelity with Michelle, it's better to leave Anna at her school while the court decides parental responsibility. The fewer changes Anna must experience at this point, the better. Kayla should also share information about their child willingly to demonstrate her intent to cooperate.

Summary

Overall, use this transition time to draw closer to your children and to care for yourself. Live in a way that presents yourself to the court as a stable, competent parent who cares for her child above all else. Follow the rules and put aside pettiness.

Call The Quick Law Group at 904-241-0012 for a consultation about your Florida divorce, or to learn more please visit TheQuickLawGroup.com.

Domestic Violence: What You Need to Know

Domestic abuse manifests in many ways: mental, emotional, physical, financial and sexual. No one deserves abuse. It is a crime. If you or your children have suffered abuse at the hands of your husband, call the police and report the situation, and talk to your attorney immediately.

Important Terms to Understand

- **"No-fault divorce":** No one is to blame for the divorce. Florida is a no-fault divorce state, meaning divorcing people do not have to state why they want to split.

- **"Fault divorce":** One or both spouses blame the other for the divorce. Florida does not recognize fault for divorce, technically, but issues such as abuse can impact child responsibility, alimony, division of assets and child support.

- **"Domestic violence":** Abuse, also known as battering, especially if physical.

- **"Protection from Abuse":** A legal order that orders your spouse away from you. If he violates the order, he may go to jail.

Mistakes Women Make Regarding Abuse and Divorce

- **Not calling the police about abuse as it happens or shortly thereafter.** Not reporting injuries to children may get you in trouble.

- **Not documenting abuse.** Take photos of injuries, damaged property, or injured children or pets. Save medical information regarding care provided for injuries. Let your attorney know of anyone who witnessed abuse or observed your injuries.

- **Not pressing charges or obtaining an order of protection.** An order of protection offers *legal* protection only. Many abusers violate orders; take steps to protect yourself.

- **Violating the order of protection by inviting the spouse over.** The court will not take the threat seriously if you don't.

- **Keeping silent.** Abuse is a crime. Do not feel ashamed for what you suffered.

- **Minimizing/excusing abuse.** Forgiveness doesn't mean forgetting about or denying that your husband committed a crime against you.

Call The Quick Law Group at 904-241-0012 for a consultation about your Florida divorce, or to learn more please visit TheQuickLawGroup.com.

Best Practices for Divorces Involving Abuse

Todd made Amber's life miserable throughout their five-year marriage. She told no one of the abuse, and they had no children. Any minor infraction of his ever-changing "rules" caused Todd to explode in anger. He threw objects at Amber and hit only where clothing hides the marks. Todd recently punched her head near her temple, resulting in a black eye. Amber realized that she could not hide his abuse; that it would only grow worse. While on her lunch break, she filed a police report and pressed charges. The police arrested Todd as his workplace. Amber filed for an order of protection and did not respond to Todd's repeated contact attempts. Amber filed for divorce and shared all of her documentation with her attorney: police report, protection order, photos, and testimonials from their next-door neighbor. She changed the locks on the house and adopted a large dog in anticipation of his release on bail. Amber's attorney feels confident that the court will award her spousal maintenance.

Summary

Abuse makes divorce even more painful; however, you must tell your attorney about what happened and share all the documentation and photos you have to receive the best settlement.

Call The Quick Law Group at 904-241-0012 for a consultation about your Florida divorce, or to learn more please visit TheQuickLawGroup.com.

Alimony in Florida: Important Terms and Ideas

Alimony refers to payments one spouse pays to the other to provide for your needs, separate from child support. Alimony is not a punishment. Either spouse may receive alimony. Since other aspects of divorce affect alimony, it's important to understand how the court arrives at an alimony settlement

Key Terms

- **Temporary.** Alimony awarded while divorce is pending.

- **Rehabilitative alimony**: Payments awarded to help the wife in becoming able to support herself. These take into account the time it will take you to complete an education or job training. A plan must be in place to ensure this type of alimony.

- **Bridge-the-gap alimony**: Helps prepare a wife for singlehood by covering expenses such as the cost of a vehicle or the price of establishing a new residence and things to "bridge" the gap between married and single life. It can only be awarded for two years.

- **Permanent alimony**: Payments last until the wife remarries or dies -- typically awarded after a long term marriage.

- **Durational alimony:** Alimony awarded for a specified time period; this is becoming more common, to eliminate permanent alimony.

- **Combination:** the court may combine different types of alimony to achieve your goals.

Common Mistakes Women Make During the Alimony Process

- **Misrepresenting finances/circumstances.** Lying hurts you once the truth is revealed.

- **Neglecting life insurance on the ex.** Suppose your ex dies? There goes alimony.

- **Low-balling alimony requests.** You're not greedy to receive what you're owed.

- **Assuming they know their husband's income.** He may hide income by accepting cash, barter, or traded items, for example, especially if he operates a business.

Call The Quick Law Group at 904-241-0012 for a consultation about your Florida divorce, or to learn more please visit TheQuickLawGroup.com.

Best Practices Regarding Alimony

While Rob worked his way up the ladder at a prestigious property management firm, Jenny quit her job to stay home with their children. She had not finished her degree, since Rob took care of the bills. He began drinking heavily. Eventually, alcohol became more important to him than anything else. Now in their 40s, they faced divorce. When then began the divorce process, Jenny felt bad about asking for alimony, since she *could* work, and she felt sure the court would award her with the house and child support. But Jenny should also consider that her job skills have become outdated since she last worked. She lacks education, too. Since they shared one vehicle, she needs help in that area as well. Jenny should not hesitate to ask for combination alimony to ensure she can support herself and the children while building a new life without Rob.

Summary

Awarding alimony does not represent a punishment to the one who pays it or a "free ride" to the recipient. Alimony helps lessen the negative financial effects of divorce for spouses who have sacrificed their own opportunities to benefit their partners.

Call The Quick Law Group at 904-241-0012 for a consultation about your Florida divorce, or to learn more please visit TheQuickLawGroup.com.

Division of Marital Property and Assets

Splitting up what you own and owe represents one of the most difficult parts of divorce. Beyond the actual worth of real estate and possessions, the emotional value can run steep. Know your rights and carefully consider what's important to you before you surrender assets.

Key Terms

- **"Property"**: Anything owned or owed by you or your spouse, including objects, money, investments, land, homes, buildings, credit card debt, and unpaid loans.

- **"Marital property"**: Assets and debts obtained while married, including spousal gifts.

- **"Non-marital/separate property"**: Assets obtained before marriage, given to one of the partners as a gift or inheritance from someone other than the spouse, or income generated by non-marital assets during the marriage (unless these funds support a spouse).

- **"Real estate"**: Land and homes or commercial buildings.

- **"Equitable distribution"**: The fair (*not necessarily equal*) division of property based upon many factors, such as: length of the marriage, contribution of each partner to the family finances and care, and who primarily cares for dependent children.

Mistakes Women Make Regarding Division of Property

- **Hiding assets.** Dishonesty counts against you when it's discovered.

- **Under- or over-estimating the value of property.**

- **Thinking that debt in only his name is his responsibility.**

- **Transferring property without an attorney's advice.**

- **Caving in to unfavorable deals based upon emotions.**

- **Basing the value of assets upon replacement value** (what it costs to buy a new one) instead of market value (what it's worth at its current condition if it were for sale now).

Call The Quick Law Group at 904-241-0012 for a consultation about your Florida divorce, or to learn more please visit TheQuickLawGroup.com.

Best Practices for Division of Property

Janette's pottery business is her "baby." Janette and her husband, David, now face divorce. They share a moderate amount of debt he was willing to take over. But David demanded that she sell her pottery studio and collection of pottery vases handed down to Janette by her grandmother. He wanted to divide the proceeds of the sale 20/80. He reasoned that most of their money had been tied up in building the business. Selling sounded like a good deal, since Janette could eliminate all her debt and keep the lion's share of the profits from the sale. Janette nearly agreed, until she spoke with her attorney. She learned that her studio, equipment, and supplies should remain untouched in division of property because they are business assets. Since she inherited the vases, she can exclude them from division of property, too. By keeping the studio, she could continue to support herself and pay off her share of the debt.

Summary

Before you agree to anything, thoroughly discuss with your attorney your complete financial picture. As your "homework," decide what is important to you, so you can present your goals to your attorney and discuss the possibilities.

Call The Quick Law Group at 904-241-0012 for a consultation about your Florida divorce, or to learn more please visit TheQuickLawGroup.com.

Litigation vs. Mediation

Couples may forgo hiring an attorney and choose mediation to settle their divorces for a variety of reasons. They may think they will save money, hasten the end of the divorce, and minimize hard feelings. Every case differs, so it's important to understand how litigation and alternatives can impact your divorce.

Key Terms

- **"Litigation"**: Settling a divorce with an attorney outside or inside court.

- **"Mediation"**: Settling an uncontested divorce out of court guided by an unbiased third party. All cases mediate: make sure you are represented during your mediation.

- **"Pro se divorce"**: Representing yourself without an attorney.

- **"Do it yourself"**: Obtaining forms and advice from non-attorney sources, such as divorce software kits.

Mistakes Women Make Regarding Litigation vs. Mediation

- **Attempting mediation for a complicated divorce without representation.**

- **Agreeing to use a mediator without being represented.**

- **Agreeing to terms they don't like** to make the divorce end quickly; not thinking of the future.

- **Representing themselves without an attorney** when their spouse has hired an attorney.

Best Practices for Litigation vs. Alternative Resolution

Diane and Rich were married for 40 years. Though his affair ended their marriage, she felt she could trust him to offer reasonable terms. She asked if they could meet with a mediator who would help them negotiate fair terms. Rich said that he did not think that was legal. Diane believed him. She did not have much money of her own, so she decided to represent herself instead of hiring an attorney. At their first meeting, she soon realized that Rich had hired an attorney who planned to clean out Diane's finances and possessions. He portrayed her as lazy for staying home with their children and making only a little money selling crafts on the side. She had little work experience and no education beyond high school. Rich had earned a degree and worked a lucrative career full time. Diane hired an attorney, who protected her from the loss,

Call The Quick Law Group at 904-241-0012 for a consultation about your Florida divorce, or to learn more please visit TheQuickLawGroup.com.

since nothing had been decided yet. As it turned out, Rich had transferred large sums of money to his girlfriend's account to hide it from Diane. But not for long. The settlement protected Diane's assets and awarded her with alimony that helped her get on her feet financially.

Summary

Your divorce may not be as simple or easy as you think. At least have an attorney review any paperwork before you sign to ensure your agreement is fair and legal. If you have any reason to question your spouse's character and honesty, hire an attorney. The money and heartache you save more than compensates for the attorney's fees you pay now.

Call The Quick Law Group at 904-241-0012 for a consultation about your Florida divorce, or to learn more please visit <u>TheQuickLawGroup.com</u>.

Child Support in Florida: Key Terms and Ideas

What about child support? Do you need it? If there's a child involved in your divorce, the simple answer is yes. Child support is an on-going payment a parent makes that contributes to a child's well being to help meet the child's needs for food, shelter and clothing. In Florida, Statute 61:30 defines the legal obligations to provide such support.

How Child Support Is Apportioned

The court will set child support based on a legal formula set by the State of Florida. Per the statute, this formula considers "all relevant factors, including the needs of the child or children, age, station in life, standard of living, and the financial status and ability of each parent."

The Florida Child Support Guidelines help the court determine total amount of money the children need. The court can modify these recommendations, but its powers are limited. The court can increase the amount by 5% or decrease it by 5% easily. To deviate further from the Guidelines, the court needs more serious reasons. For instance, maybe the child has a serious medical condition and needs to take costly medicines every day. Or maybe you (or your husband) plans to spend a lopsided amount of time taking care of the kids. In order for the court to deviate, the evidence must be substantial.

Best Practices for Child Support

While common mistakes can occur during the child support process, most can be avoided:

- **Understand your financial needs and options.** Establish a clear budget for yourself and your financial priorities, so you can handle whatever happens.

- **Protect your children's welfare.** Use support payments for your children's needs, such as food, clothing, medical costs, and shelter.

- **Set up child support early in the divorce.** Receive payments through direct deposit -- do not depend on your husband sending checks.

- **Intervene quickly if payments aren't made.**

Call The Quick Law Group at 904-241-0012 for a consultation about your Florida divorce, or to learn more please visit TheQuickLawGroup.com.

A Story to Illustrate What Might Happen in a Child Support Case

Lola decided she could raise her child on her own, and she didn't ask for child support. A year after her divorce, however, a job change lowered her income. She felt bad about asking her former husband for help, because she knew he was struggling financially, too, and because she'd begun dating, and he hadn't. Nevertheless, Lola knew that she needed to do what was in the best interest of her child. Unfortunately, her ex refused to pay. She then sought the help of the court to garnish his wages. He complied with the obligation, but the drawn out, emotionally draining process left both Lola and her husband angry with each other and exhausted.

The moral is this: avoid treating your child support case lightly. Invest time and energy into protecting your and your children's financial needs early in the process to save everyone involved heartache and frustration.

Call The Quick Law Group at 904-241-0012 for a consultation about your Florida divorce, or to learn more please visit TheQuickLawGroup.com.

FAQs About Divorce in Florida

What do you need to do to get a divorce in Florida?

The law says that the marriage must be "irretrievably broken" -- a rather loose definition. Both spouses don't have to agree to divorce; either spouse can make the call unilaterally. You do not have to show that there was any violence or adultery or other problems. But either you or your husband must have been Florida residents for six months prior to the filing of the petition.

What's the first step that generally happens in the process?

You file a petition for Dissolution of Marriage. This describes your claims regarding elements like alimony, property distribution, time sharing, etc. Then you serve your papers to the other spouse. If you have children in the marriage, you will need to complete a seminar that provides insight about how to care for children during a divorce.

How long will the process take?

Generally 9-12 months. This considers many factors, including:

- Whether or not you and your husband can agree on key terms of settlement;
- Whether you can negotiate a resolution or whether you need to go to litigation;
- The size and complexity of the marital estate;
- The duration of the marriage;
- How hard both sides are willing to fight to get what they want;
- Quality and disposition of the attorneys who represent both spouses;

On the quick end, you may be able to complete an uncontested divorce in as little as three months. That means that you and your husband basically agree on everything. If the court needs to decide on issues, you may have to wait several months before your case even is heard.

Do I really need a lawyer to represent me?

Yes. Florida divorce is a complex process. Even seemingly simple, mundane cases have a way of taking strange turns. Let's say you and your husband agree on all the terms now. You still can't predict what you might say or do weeks from now or what additional demands he might make. Plus, self-representation exposes you to many risks, which can reverberate in your life (and your kids' lives) for years. In some ways, opting to be your own lawyer in a divorce would be like opting to be your own surgeon: you would be taking on a high risk endeavor without training. Our office focuses only on family law; our experience will guide you through the process.

Call The Quick Law Group at 904-241-0012 for a consultation about your Florida divorce, or to learn more please visit TheQuickLawGroup.com.

How can I speed up and streamline the process – to minimize having to go to court and spend a lot of money and time?

Organization is key! Get clear about the values that you want to govern the divorce and your ideal endpoints. What do you want to be true, once everything is finalized? How do you want to feel about the process? What would be unacceptable? What behaviors, actions, etc. do you want to avoid? The more issues that you can resolve peaceably early on, the smoother the process will be. Don't expect to negotiate everything to a fine point in the first few conversations.

Strive for success not just on your terms but also on your husband's terms. Try to identify the needs buried underneath his demands. And then invent ways to meet those needs while respecting your own needs. For instance, let's say that, while you're dividing up your marital property, you encounter a rare set of expensive flatware that you both received as a wedding gift. You suggest splitting the flatware up, 50/50. But he wants to take it all, because the flatware was a gift from his late grandmother. He wants it for sentimental reasons. You have a need for equitable distribution of your property. He has a need to retain a vibrant connection to his past. Recognizing these two needs, you might suggest a compromise position: he can keep all the flatware, as long as you can take other assets (such as artwork) of similar value. That way you split the value of the property equally AND he keeps what's sentimentally important to him.

Be on the lookout for these "win-win" opportunities, and you'll be more likely to resolve your divorce faster and smoother.

What if my husband hit me? What if he threatens me? Should I call my attorney?

If you or your kids are in danger, *call the police*. First and foremost, protect yourself and your children. Once you have gotten to safety, call your attorney, who can help you by applying for a restraining order or other legal protections. Depending on what happened, your attorney may be able to help you remove your husband from the house. Document evidence of what happened. For instance, journal about what happened, take pictures of any bruising or injuries, and collect witness statements. The court considers domestic violence issues high priority. So even if your actual divorce filing may take months to resolve, you won't have to wait months to calm the situation and stay safe, if he's been abusive towards you and/or your children.

What if my husband won't pay child support or alimony? What if he keeps control of the house or of our bank accounts?

During the divorce, the court can and does order temporary alimony and child support. Depending on circumstances, you may be able to ask the court to force distribution of assets or provide other types of relief, such as alimony or child support.

Call The Quick Law Group at 904-241-0012 for a consultation about your Florida divorce, or to learn more please visit TheQuickLawGroup.com.

When can alimony amounts be changed?

Florida Statute 61.14 says that alimony (both durational and rehabilitative) can be altered, provided that you can show that there has been a "substantial change in circumstances." This might mean that your situation has changed – for instance, maybe you lost your job or got socked with a massive medical bill. The court may also terminate or modify alimony if you (or your husband) remarries or cohabitates with someone who provides financial support. The burden of proof is high, which is why the initial divorce matters so much.

Is mediation a good option for me?

Mediation is required in all divorces in Florida. It is very useful, since it's often faster, less messy, and more "win-win" oriented than litigation. During mediation, skilled negotiating partners help you and your spouse work out elements of the settlement. These mutual parties can help you and your husband work out the kinks of the arrangement and avoid misunderstandings, petty fights, etc. Before you proceed with mediation, you need to go through a comprehensive discovery process. Basically, you and your husband will exchange financial documents to reveal exactly what's going on with your finances and marital assets. You want "all the cards on the table," metaphorically speaking.

What if my husband hides income or engages in other financial shenanigans to get out of paying child support, alimony, etc.?

You have the burden to show that he is hiding money or making money under the table. If he's guilty of engaging in these practices, he could face civil and perhaps criminal charges as well as negative repercussions with respect to the divorce. The court can also order wage garnishments – i.e., money could be taken directly out of his paycheck to pay support and/or alimony.

What if my husband refuses to let me see my kids? Can I refuse to let him to the kids, in turn? What are my options?

Parenting plans are not optional. You can ask the court to order time-sharing immediately. If your husband refuses, he could be held in contempt and face charges. In general, avoid a "tit for tat" mentality. Talk to your lawyer and ask the court to help you obtain relief. Always seek the additional advice of a mental health provider.

What if I want to move out of Florida? What if my husband wants to move?

Relocation is a complex, tricky issue. If you or your husband wants to move 50+ plus miles away, the courts consider that move a "relocation." If you fail to follow statutory guidelines for relocation with children, you can face penalties, such as contempt and other charges. The court may prohibit relocation, delay it, or allow it temporarily. The non-relocating spouse may need to share costs, including transportation costs, and ensure that people can communicate – via the

Call The Quick Law Group at 904-241-0012 for a consultation about your Florida divorce, or to learn more please visit TheQuickLawGroup.com.

phone, the web, etc. – enough to meet the needs of the parenting plan.

Is there a Statute of Limitations for child support in Florida?

No, but in the event of a major delay, a legal idea called "laches" comes into play. Basically, the court will take the lengthy delay into account when determining the child support arrangement.

How will the marital assets be divided up?

In Florida, marital properties are equitably divided, beginning with a 50/50 arrangement. Likewise, the court will typically divide the marital debts in half as well. The court is generally not interested in a close itemization of who racked up which debts and why -- i.e. who bought what shoes and who spent how much on which golf clubs. For instance, if you inherited property or received a gift in your name from another person, like your aunt or an old employer, those assets should not be split up in a 50/50 manner. Your attorney can help you assess the financial landscape and make intelligent decisions.

What if I have more questions that I need to answer?

This list of FAQs only scratches the surface about what you want to know about alimony, child support, distribution of assets, the length of the process, etc. To keep yourself sane and focused, create a worksheet at home listing all the pressing questions you have. Whenever a new question pops up in your mind -- whether it happens at 4 in the morning or on vacation -- jot a note down about it, and then later add it to your list. Later on, "batch ask" these questions to your attorney. This process can save both you time and energy and reduce your legal bills. It will also leave you feeling in control, since you won't have to worry about "loose questions" rattling around in your head. Document these questions and answers for easy referral. You're also welcome to call our offices at **904-241-0012** for clarification or for resources to handle any divorce-related challenge.

Call The Quick Law Group at 904-241-0012 for a consultation about your Florida divorce, or to learn more please visit TheQuickLawGroup.com.

Using the "5 Whys" to Understand the Roots of Your Divorce-Related Problems

The more clarity you have about what you want from the divorce process -- and what you don't want -- the simpler things will be, and the more likely you are to be satisfied with the outcome.

Here's a great exercise to get clarity about what's holding you back. The strategy is called the "5 Whys." Japanese engineers pioneered this technique to identify the true root causes of problems to solve them better. Here's a metaphor to explain why this thinking is useful:

Imagine that water is leaking through your car's windows. Also, the brakes don't work. And the ignition won't turn. And the floor mats are sopping wet. You could hire a mechanic to check your brakes and engine and invest hundreds of dollars in new floor mats and windows. But all that effort won't mean much if the root problem is that *your car is floating in the swimming pool!*

The moral is: you need to understand what the REAL problem is (regarding your divorce or any other big issue in your life) if you want to make lasting, effective progress.

The 5 Whys exercise helps you drill down to find out what's really wrong. Here's how it works. Start with any divorce-related problem. Then ask yourself "why is this happening?" When you answer that question, next ask "well, what's causing *that*?" Proceed in this manner, drilling down using "why questions" until you find the true root cause.

Let's do an example.

Perhaps you have no idea how much money is in your marital estate. You're worried because finances are not your strong suit. You want to make sure your husband isn't hiding assets from you, etc. Here's how the exercise might proceed.

Why #1: "Why don't I have more detailed knowledge about our family finances?"
Answer #1: "Because I trusted my husband to take care of the bills and household finances."

Why #2. "Why did I trust my husband with the bills and household finances?"
Answer #2: "Because I'm not talented at accounting or interested in finances."

Why #3: "Why am I not skilled or interested in finances?"
Answer #3: "Because I struggled with math in school and never learned how to do a budget."

Why #4: "Why did I struggle in school with these topics?"
Answer #4: "Because I didn't get enough support from other people."

Call The Quick Law Group at 904-241-0012 for a consultation about your Florida divorce, or to learn more please visit TheQuickLawGroup.com.

Why #5: "Why didn't I get enough support?"
Answer #5: "Because I just fundamentally have a hard time asking for what I want and being assertive about it."

Now we are at the root cause! This exercise revealed something fundamental about the person -- her lack of assertiveness -- that indirectly caused the financial-records issue. With that kind of insight, you can quickly solve very deep but critical problems in your life and relationships.

Call The Quick Law Group at 904-241-0012 for a consultation about your Florida divorce, or to learn more please visit TheQuickLawGroup.com.

Feel More Energized and Healthy By Improving Your Diet

Few experiences cause more physical and emotional stress than divorce. Stress negatively impacts many systems of the body, including blood pressure and metabolism. Add to that the typical American diet of sugary, processed foods, and you may find yourself teetering from average health into disease--literally, "dis-ease."

Changing what you eat can help improve your health in many ways; however, the media floods women with conflicting messages about what's good for them and what's not. For example, one minute eggs are cholesterol bombs that curse you with heart disease. Then a new study says that eggs are miracle foods, packed with choline and other key nutrients. Every person's metabolism and genetic make-up makes her unique. But good eating habits serve everyone well.

- Focus on eating real food, including nutrient dense fruits and vegetables; healthy proteins; and healthy fats.

- Eat a colorful diet. Dark or vibrant-colored fruits and vegetables tend to provide the most nutrients.

- Avoid or limit eating processed grains, such as white bread, white rice and white pasta, which have been stripped of many nutrients and which spike blood sugar and insulin.

- Avoid or limit sugar consumption. (Here's a detailed, technical explanation why.)

- Powerful evidence suggests that many people who suffer from obesity, diabetes or metabolic syndrome may benefit from some form of therapeutic dietary carbohydrate restriction. See this link for a summary of relevant science.

- Eat plenty of natural health fat, including both monounsaturated fat (found in olive oil) AND saturated fat found in natural foods like butter, coconut oil and lard. Saturated fat is no longer something to be feared. According to a massive meta-analysis (study of studies) published early in 2014 in the Annals of Internal Medicine, saturated fat does not cause heart disease. Per a New York Times report on the study: "a large and exhaustive new analysis by a team of international scientists found no evidence that eating saturated fat increased heart attacks and other cardiac events." This echoed another major meta-analysis conducted in 2010, which also found "no significant evidence for concluding that dietary saturated fat is associated with an increased risk of CHD or CVD."

- Do not worry about restricting salt, unless you're salt sensitive.

Call The Quick Law Group at 904-241-0012 for a consultation about your Florida divorce, or to learn more please visit TheQuickLawGroup.com.

- Do not bother counting calories for weight loss. This strategy doesn't work, and it's fundamentally nonsensical, as science journalist <u>Gary Taubes explains in this video</u>. The key to weight management is the management of hormones -- in particular, the hormone insulin.

Summary

Of course, no one eats properly all the time. "Falling off the wagon" happens to everyone, but you diet and nutrition can play a profound role in your health. Educate yourself, and make sure you work with your doctor to find a plan that works for you.

Call The Quick Law Group at 904-241-0012 for a consultation about your Florida divorce, or to learn more please visit <u>TheQuickLawGroup.com</u>.

Get Calmer and Reduce Anxiety by Practicing Mindfulness

What Is Mindfulness?

Mindfulness is an old spiritual tradition with roots in Buddhist meditation. It's currently gaining in popularity throughout the U.S. The goal of the practice is to maintain moment to moment awareness of thoughts, feelings, your body and the world around you.

But why do this?

Mindfulness is fundamentally about acceptance -- about accepting your own thoughts and feelings, without worrying whether they're right or wrong. By living in the present, you won't be thinking about past wrongs or worrying about the future. And that's a good way to stay calm during your divorce. Mindfulness is also good for your mind. Powerful science suggests it can reduce depression and stress and increases positive emotions and affect. It's good for the body, too. A recent study showed that people who practiced meditation for eight weeks enjoyed enhanced immune system functioning.

How to Be Mindful

First, make time in your day to be mindful -- start with just 15 to 20 minutes a day. Practice either first thing in the morning or before you go to sleep at night. Set up an area of your room with a comfortable pillow to sit on -- a clean, quiet space. If you have children, let them know not to interrupt you. Turn off your phone and your computer.

You can start the process by breathing in and out, watching the breath. You don't need to force the breath -- just pay attention to its sensation going in and out of your body. Whenever your mind wanders (and wander it will!) gently acknowledge that you've lost focus, and put your attention back on the breath. Keep this up for the whole session -- that's all there is to it!

You can also check out mindfulness websites, podcasts, and guided mindfulness sessions on YouTube to learn more or aid your practice.

How Mindfulness Can Help

Anna couldn't stop obsessing about her divorce -- and about how callously her husband had acted towards the end of their relationship. The thoughts were distracting her at work and making her depressed. Practicing mindfulness every morning helped her tune out those bad feelings and thoughts. Her memory and attention improved, and work became much easier.

Marie felt impatient with her children and reluctant to help her co-workers. Mindfulness gave her **Call The Quick Law Group at 904-241-0012 for a consultation about your Florida divorce, or to learn more please visit TheQuickLawGroup.com.**

a new sense of understanding about the problems of others. She felt more compassionate and empathetic towards her children, her co-workers and herself.

Susan found that practicing mindfulness made her feel happier about her parenting. She relaxed and enjoyed her children more, instead of struggling to make them feel better about the divorce.

Want to Learn More about Mindfulness

Check out these interesting links:

- http://www.mindfulness.com.au/Mindfulness%20explained.htm
- http://www.psychologytoday.com/blog/the-mindful-self-express/201202/nine-essential-qualities-mindfulness

Call The Quick Law Group at 904-241-0012 for a consultation about your Florida divorce, or to learn more please visit TheQuickLawGroup.com.

Obtaining Social Support

Whether you were married for 3 months or 30 years, you no doubt came to rely on your husband for companionship, guidance and empathy. Now that you're separated, your primary confidant is no longer available to advise you or listen to what's going on in your life.

Human beings are social creatures. We need to be around other people – for many reasons:

- We have needs to be touched, physically, by other people;
- We have needs to be heard and understood by others;
- Being around supportive people can have positive effects on our stress levels, health, wellbeing, and outlook on life;
- We rely on other people to solve diverse problems in our complex modern world.

Unfortunately, after a breakup, many women intuitively retreat into isolation or semi-isolation. Some degree of introspection is no doubt fine… and even a bit healthy. And some people are simply more introverted than others -- i.e. they don't need the same degree of social stimulation as other people do. However, it's easy to fall into destructive cycle: first, you fail to meet your social needs; then, this isolation feeds on itself and makes you less likely to seek support. And so on and so forth.

So how do you break this cycle?

First, take initiative and be purposeful about seeking social support. Don't expect things to happen on their own. Schedule appointments and social dates. Be mindful of social needs that are not being met. Know thyself! Once you know what you're missing, get creative to solve the issue. For instance, let's sue you're really needing touch and companionship. Consider getting a dog or a cat. Or volunteer to babysit for a friend who needs childcare. Alternatively, maybe you just need someone to talk to -- if so, join a support group or reach out to friends and family.

Dating

Here are a few other big, related questions:

- When should you date?
- How should you approach the dating process?
- Is an online dating a good way to go, or should you get referrals from friends?

The bottom line is: if/when you're ready to date, proceed with caution. Avoid revealing a lot of information about your divorce, and avoid getting into an intense "rebound" situation right off the bat. First, get a handle on your divorce before you complexify your life, your world -- and potentially your relationship with your children -- with another new relationship.

Call The Quick Law Group at 904-241-0012 for a consultation about your Florida divorce, or to learn more please visit TheQuickLawGroup.com.

Divorce's Effects on Children

Divorce, in and of itself, generally does not harm children, over the long run. [During the first three years after the split, they may experience emotional challenges and trouble at school.] Family instability -- rather than the divorce itself -- may be the real danger. Sociologist Andrew Cherlin argues in his book, The Marriage-Go-Round, that rapid re-partnering after a divorce could be more harmful to kids than the separation itself. To that end, avoid cycling partners into your life and your home.

Call The Quick Law Group at 904-241-0012 for a consultation about your Florida divorce, or to learn more please visit TheQuickLawGroup.com.

Journaling

The art and science of journaling is profound – and potentially profoundly useful. If you don't keep a journal, consider starting one. If you do, consider expanding its utility to address your divorce-related concerns. Try some or all of the following journaling exercises.

1. Give gratitude.

Surprisingly powerful research suggests that journaling gratitude everyday can have positive, long-lasting effects on your level of happiness. Here's what you do. In your journal, every night, write down three things that happened to you that day that filled you with gratitude. These can be small things -- such as the sight of the sand on a beach or a kind word a stranger said to you. Or they can be large things -- such as a sense of wonder evoked by looking into the eyes of your young child. Just write down what made you grateful and how you felt. Try to physically recall the good feelings in your body.

Do this every day, and science says that you will become a happier person.

2. Reflect on your strengths and stretches. What challenges you? How and when do you excel, and why?

Most people are not taught to get clear about who they are and what they want in life. They don't understand their true strengths and weaknesses. A lack of self-knowledge can be a dangerous thing. So cultivate self-knowledge by exploring the following ideas in your journal:

- What are you good at?
- What are you bad at?
- What do you love to do?
- What you struggle to do?

Ask these questions repeatedly, and you'll quickly see patterns in your life and in your relationships. You can use that knowledge to make positive changes -- to stop doing things that don't bring you joy and start doing things that actually do.

3. Do a weekly Q&A with yourself.

Develop a list of "questions and answers" that you fill in every week to keep you grounded and focused on achieving great things. Here are some sample questions:

- What are three things I'm really proud that I did this week?
- What are my top goals for next week?
- I am really looking forward to the finalization of the divorce because [fill in the blank].

Call The Quick Law Group at 904-241-0012 for a consultation about your Florida divorce, or to learn more please visit TheQuickLawGroup.com.

- I really regretted doing [fill in the blank] last week.
- If next week was my last week to live, I would make sure to do [fill in the blank].
- Once big lesson I learned from my divorce is [fill in the blank].

4. Use "if then" statements to break bad habits in your relationship and in your life.

Our bad habits, beliefs, and thoughts often get in the way of our success. But how do you break out of old, unsuccessful ways of dealing with yourself and with the world?

Here's a powerful tool to recalibrate. It's called the "if/then" exercise. Basically, you consciously reprogram how you automatically think/act/react by developing contingency plans, based on situations that you regularly encounter.

That may sound abstract, so let's work through an example.

Michelle is 38-year-old graphic designer who just separated from her husband of nine years, Jim. They have two small kids together, and they fight a lot about how to take care of them. Emily often struggles with her temper, and shouts at Jim... and sometimes at the kids. She'd really like to fix this behavior, since it harmed her relationship, and she can see that it could cause problems with her kids.

So what does she do?

First, Michelle *identifies situations that trigger her angry, reactive behavior*. For instance, maybe she fumes when she's tired or overworked or when she hasn't eaten well. To deal with these triggers for her "mad mom" reflexes, Emily constructs the following contingences:

- "**If** I sleep less than 7 hours in a night, **then** I will take a break from work and take a nap or make sure to go to bed half-an-hour early in the evening."
- "**If** work really stresses me out, **then** I will find 15 minutes to sit and meditate to calm down or talk on the phone with my best friend, Kathy, to talk me off the ledge."
- "**If** I haven't eaten a healthy meal in a while, **then** I will stop what I'm doing and have a hardboiled egg or string cheese – some good, healthy, protein rich food that does not give me a blood sugar crash or stimulate junk food cravings."

The "if/then" exercise aims to identify concrete, actionable steps that you can take to promote better behavior. Try it yourself! Identify your most pressing, urgent, personal crisis, and come up with contingency plans (like Emily did) to stop your problems before they start.

Call The Quick Law Group at 904-241-0012 for a consultation about your Florida divorce, or to learn more please visit TheQuickLawGroup.com.

Get Organized and Clearheaded

Regardless of the reason behind your divorce, you have a lot going on in your life right now. Your home and thoughts can tumble into chaos, right at the time when you need orderliness to make wise decisions. In his bestselling book, *Getting Things Done*, efficiency author David Allen describes techniques that can enhance your ability to function during your divorce. Allen blames misplaced "stuff" for getting people off track.

He writes, "Here's how I define 'stuff': anything you have allowed into your psychological or physical world that doesn't belong where it is, but for which you haven't yet determined the desired outcome and the next action step" [*Getting Things Done*, pg. 17].

"Stuff" saps energy and wastes time. Whether it's seething over an email, or feeling overwhelmed by piles of objects you must sort, too much stuff draws your attention away from what's important. During your divorce, you must protect and nurture yourself and your children.

The Getting Things Done (GTD) method involves categorizing stuff as either things you should get rid of (both thoughts and physical things) or as things about which you need to take action. Then you put stuff where it belongs. Allen describes the process on www.gettingthingsdone.com as: "(1), Capture–collect what has your attention, (2) Clarify–process what it means, (3) Organize–put it where it belongs, (4) Reflect–review frequently, and (5) Engage–simply do."

Example of Applying "Getting Things Done" Principles During a Divorce to Get Clarity

During her divorce, Marie dreaded doing anything with the photos and mementos of vacations she and her husband, Vince, had taken. She spent lots of time weighing what she should do about the albums and mementos on her shelves. Facing a move, she also delayed packing it all.

Fortunately, Marie understood the gist of the GTD process and used it to regain control.

First, she clarified to herself that disliked doing anything with the items because they dredged up memories of Vince's abuse. Despite him, Marie had enjoyed visiting the Rockies, touring the Finger Lakes Wine Country and all their other trips. She did not want to toss the good memories.

Next, Diane, a trusted friend, helped Marie organize the items into two groups: what she didn't want and the memorabilia which she really enjoyed and would use: a cheeseboard she had selected from a Finger Lakes winery and a woven rug from a shop in the Rockies. Neither evoked sad memories. Diane helped her sell the other trip trinkets online. With the proceeds, she paid for some moving expenses, releasing more stress. Diane also helped purge Vince's photos. Only the scenic ones remained. They then consolidated the photos into fewer, new albums. Her house felt more spacious, and the new albums symbolized her emerging, new life. By using GTD techniques, Marie pruned both mental and physical stuff. Throughout her divorce, she reviewed the mental and physical stuff in her life and put it where it belonged.

Call The Quick Law Group at 904-241-0012 for a consultation about your Florida divorce, or to learn more please visit TheQuickLawGroup.com.

Using GTD to Sort Email During/After Your Divorce

E-mails often seem more urgent than they really are. Full inboxes generate stress by affirming you're getting nothing done. And agonizing over what to do with the messages creates more stress and squanders more time. An articles by Samphy Y at www.worklifepointers.com recommends using David Allen's "4 D's" to decide how to deal with e-mail:

- **Do it** - if you can respond in two minutes to the request for end of year stub, send it.
- **Delegate it** - if your tax preparer can find that 1099 faster than you, forward the request.
- **Defer it** - if you don't have time right now to answer your sister's lengthy letter, put it off.
- **Dump it** - cute stories, funny pictures and non-helpful information just wastes time.

Call The Quick Law Group at 904-241-0012 for a consultation about your Florida divorce, or to learn more please visit TheQuickLawGroup.com.

Interview with Heather Quick

What got you excited about working with people who are going through divorce?

I used to work for a criminal prosecutor, and we did a lot of litigation. As I learned from him and became more involved in the process, I recognized a need for courtroom skills and litigation in family law. I am blessed to be happily married, but my parents have actually been divorced more than once. So I've had a lot of experience with divorce from that perspective.

After I started in family law, I realized that the clients that I get the most satisfaction from helping are women, because I see women sacrifice so much in divorce. And sometimes they'll make unnecessary compromises.

Why do women make those compromises? Is it cultural? What causes that?

I've seen it in so many clients… a lot of times, it's the children.

What about the children?

Women might think to themselves "Oh! My children are suffering, I just want this to be done, for their sakes." Overall, women have very strong bonds with their children. More often than not, children remain with their moms during the process. And sometimes the children can feel sympathetic for their dads: "Oh, poor dad, don't be so lonely… he has no money."

Or sometimes the women are very angry… but then they think "well, maybe we should just settle." And I'm not against mediation or settling, because it's always better to save money and avoid animosity over the long term. But there are some things women shouldn't sacrifice.

What do they intuitively want to sacrifice that you feel they should not?

Money.

Because they want to be finished with the divorce, and so they compromise?

Yes, this is really evident in the following situation: a high earning couple owns substantial assets that must be split, but the woman either doesn't earn or earns substantially less than the husband does. She's ready to be done now with the divorce process. So she settles for less than she should get. But in a year or two or three, she comes to regret this.

Sounds like a lot of women just want to get control over their lives, but in searching for compromise, they wind up short changing themselves.

Call The Quick Law Group at 904-241-0012 for a consultation about your Florida divorce, or to learn more please visit TheQuickLawGroup.com.

That's true. There's so much emotion involved in divorce.

At the end of the day, it's the one who has the most resolve during the negotiations that prevails. I tell my clients to hold out: let me do this for you -- be strong for you. In the end, they're glad.

Do you think a fear of the financial impact of divorce traps some women into remaining in a marriage that they know they should leave?

Absolutely. The financial situation has a huge impact. It's scary, particularly when you don't have skills or the education, and you just don't really know what's going to happen. You also just don't know what the marital assets are, and so you get scared and embarrassed. So many times, I've heard clients tell me *"I don't even know what things cost to run the house!"*

Right.

There's nothing embarrassing about that. In most households, one person typically tends to the finances. Very often, the woman knows everything -- knows the numbers. Sometimes the husband does. In either case, women can find the split scary because of creature comforts they have to leave behind. And the reality is, they're not going to live exactly the same lifestyle, because at the end of the day, there is still one income and now two households. You may get 50% of the assets, but the support -- while the man may find it shockingly high, it's not going to be high. So it's scary to give up the lifestyle.

The social aspect is key, too. Because we're influenced by our social circles. And some women will stay in something that maybe they feel isn't working. But they're just not ready. I don't encourage divorce unless there's a safety issue. Then I say: *you need to make some changes.*

Making the decision is hard because there's always going to be a holiday, a birthday, a graduation, a wedding, grandchildren… there's always something!

With women who are unhappy in their 40s and on the fence… I remind them it's going to be a lot harder to split up when you're in your 60s. But they have to make that personal decision as to what they are willing to keep in their life and what they're going to give up.

It also seems like there's a sense of inertia: you're safe, you're comfortable, you have friends, you have money, you can go on vacations. But at the same time, you're fundamentally unhappy with the relationship, maybe the husband cheated or did something terrible. Many of these women must feel a deep conflict about what to do.

I certainly encourage clients to talk to a counselor if they're conflicted, because it's going to be a big decision either way. Usually, women think for a long time before they actually make that bold move to talk to a divorce attorney. But riding the fence can be stressful. If you're living in a state of not knowing, I think that makes people very uncomfortable.

Call The Quick Law Group at 904-241-0012 for a consultation about your Florida divorce, or to learn more please visit TheQuickLawGroup.com.

Right.

And many clients don't even know their rights: *"I had no idea I could get alimony!"*

There are hard choices to make… and so many options. Sometimes, women stay because they think staying will help their kids. But if mom is not happy, no one is happy. When you make better choices for you, your kids will thrive.

Does divorce, in your experience, challenge children? Can kids thrive after divorce?

The support system the kids can access plays a huge role -- families, community, churches. But when a client tells me *"I don't want to split up because of the kids,"* I have to ask them -- what do you think it's doing to your daughter to watch you in a relationship where there is no affection?

What is that teaching her about marriage? What is that teaching your son about marriage that you two scream at each other all the time? Those are hard, painful questions. But children are so perceptive -- they know what's going on. Many times the kids are relieved, actually: "Finally, mom, you're doing something!"

But as a parent myself, I know it would be absolutely heartbreaking to tell them. So I certainly know these are not light decisions.

Earlier you said you experienced divorce as a child yourself. Your parents split up. Does that experience inform how you talk to your clients and how you're able to relate to them?

At first it was hard, but I think it has enabled me to adapt and do things that I otherwise wouldn't. We try to make our children's lives absolutely perfect. But children have a deep ability to cope. Look at people who have achieved great things -- they always struggle.

When there are issues with children, I refer clients always to a psychologist and family therapist, so that they can really get solid advice from someone who's trained to handle the issues.

Can you talk about your general process? What does it entail to work with a divorce attorney like you?

When the client comes into the office, we do some pre-questioning and give them information about us. Then I meet with them in a consultation. The purpose of the initial consultation for me is probably different than what they think it is. When they come in, they are interviewing lawyers, and they want to get questions answered. People Google everything, and they have all these ideas about what divorce is and is not. But my goal in the initial consultation is to develop a relationship with the person, because we're going to be handling the hardest thing they've ever done. It's very personal, very private, and developing the relationship is probably the most

Call The Quick Law Group at 904-241-0012 for a consultation about your Florida divorce, or to learn more please visit TheQuickLawGroup.com.

important thing because trust is such a big issue. And I have my own belief system and morals and ethics, and they have to be compatible. If we're not aligned with where a person is, morally and ethically, then we're not going to represent them.

What would be an example of a non-alignment?

If a person wants us to do things -- use the kids to manipulate an outcome, for instance. It's very rare, but I have had to tell people it's not going to be a good fit.

The point is, I really want to know what their goal is. And a lot of them say *"I don't know,"* but really they do. They know what they want.

Really?

The consultation is an opportunity to get a sense of who they are -- and for them to get a sense of who we are. They sometimes ask: *"oh, I want to know every scenario..."* and that's just not what we do in an initial meeting. We develop a relationship. Are we going to be able to work together? Do we have compatibility, so that we can work together and I can achieve your goals?

And then we move forward with our process and develop their strategy.

In cases where they're not quite sure about finances, they may not know everything that's gone on. We may encourage them to do some snooping to find out... We also encourage them to work with financial planners. Just try to find out as much as you can first. A big part of divorce is not anything jazzy or sexy. It's getting things documented.

And many women need to consider: *what will it cost you? Is it feasible to remain in this house?* Perhaps there's enough money for you to stay there. But there is a lot of "pre-work" to do.

And if you don't do this "pre-work" preparation, and the case ends up going to trial, what happens then?

Sometimes, you wind up chasing down the information a bit more, and it just takes time. And, of course, everybody wants their divorce done tomorrow. And I get that! No one has ever complained to me that their divorce moved too quickly. It's a long process and it's frustrating.

The document wrangling takes time... and often, in litigation, they don't see anything happening. It's not often that you're going to court -- you're just getting and moving documents. That can be extremely frustrating for the client. That's why, the more financial information we have, the better.

Call The Quick Law Group at 904-241-0012 for a consultation about your Florida divorce, or to learn more please visit TheQuickLawGroup.com.

What about safety issues, like domestic violence?

I've met women who are in truly abusive relationships -- who are really scared. Whether it's emotional or verbal abuse, there's a lot of fear involved. And so I really try to empower them: *we can do this and get you in a better situation.*

What are the biggest worries these women face? Is it the financial stuff? Are they worried about their kids? Their safety? Everything at once?

It varies. A psychologist once told me, when folks go through divorce, they go through temporary insanity. I mean, they say things they never expected to say, they do things they never expected to do... And there's a lot of immediate financial focus: *okay, we're going to file, what are they going do? Will he try to cancel my credit cards?*

There is some protection. You can't cancel health insurance. You can't deplete bank accounts or cancel credit cards and not pay the bills you could pay. So there are some safeguards. But you still have to be aware, and people will still do all kinds of things. With women, the financial issues are certainly a big deal. If all they use is a debit card or credit card, and it doesn't work... that's a real concern. And there tends to always be a period of some bad behavior.

In almost every divorce? Really?

Yeah. Sometimes it's just a little bit. And some days are worse than others. But I tell clients all the time: *this is a marathon; you've got to pace yourself.* At the end of the day, things will tend to even out.

So it seems like it gets crazy at the beginning, but then things generally calm down?

Yes. And I've said this before: *it's going to get worse before it gets better.* And the client is like: *what are you talking about, how it can ever be worse than this?*
On the other hand, even if something starts off badly, it can get to a more mellow point. A lot depends on the choice of attorney. But it can be tough. He may hate you for leaving. He may say a lot of mean things and truly believe them. Maybe he's just a mean person, and that's why she's leaving him.

It sounds incredibly challenging. It's cool that you're there to help people, guide them through the chaos. Do you keep in touch with your clients, once the storm has cleared?

That's something we're really working towards, because as we build the practice, we're able to help more and more clients. When I started out, it was just me. So there is only so much one person can do. Now, with more staff, we can do a lot more.

Call The Quick Law Group at 904-241-0012 for a consultation about your Florida divorce, or to learn more please visit TheQuickLawGroup.com.

There's no doubt that there is going to be life after this. If you look at it in a positive way, a divorce can be a growing experience. If you haven't had a job in years, you can retrain... It's an opportunity to start anew, maybe have a new career or education... there are many opportunities.

A great positive from clients is that they are remarrying. It means they didn't lose hope and found love. I find that inspiring.

Before we wrap up... here's one thing I think is important to address: there are a lot of divorce attorneys in Jacksonville and in Florida. What sets you apart?

We are not afraid to go to court and really go after what our clients deserve. It's easy to get lost in the legal process, so you have to be aggressive to push your case through, to get things moving. It requires will and a strong desire to do that. And I feel like we're very proactive in moving cases along, settling things and getting before a judge.

My approach is to keep cases moving forward, going to court, getting things done. And then there is client education, obviously. They need to understand: *this is what we're going to do. This is why we're doing it. This is what we think will happen.*

At the same time, I learned a long time ago to ask what clients want, instead of presuming to know. Everybody has different goals. It's very important that you ask: *what do you want? Where do you want to be?* And so, we really are client-driven, because everybody is very unique, their cases are unique, and they need to be treated in that way honors that uniqueness.

I also advocate bringing in other professionals to assist us. I am certainly not an accountant, so when we need an accountant or financial planner or counselor, we get the needed help from great people we know and trust. I've really developed a strong network of referrals for our clients.

We're also very helpful with clients getting them ready to testify, because the judge needs to hear certain things. And what you intuitively want to say will not be what the judge wants to hear.

Also, while you're going through the process, you may change what you want. You know, you may be trying so hard to win the house, and then maybe you realize, ultimately, it's not where you want to live.

As Dwight Eisenhower said: planning is essential, but plans are useless. Once you set a goal, you need to adjust the process based on feedback and your experiences.

That's true. And that's what's special about being a divorce attorney – developing relationships with clients to help them respond to these big changes in a strategic, thoughtful way.

Call The Quick Law Group at 904-241-0012 for a consultation about your Florida divorce, or to learn more please visit TheQuickLawGroup.com.

Conclusion

The Florida divorce process is neither easy, nor intuitive. And that's too bad. You likely have already gone through complicated, difficult times. Undoubtedly, you'll face more challenges (emotional, physical, and financial) in the weeks and months to come.

However, you don't have to go through this process by yourself!

My team and I are here for you to help you understand not only the step-by-step process that you need to go through to get the results you want, but also to provide supportive, empathetic guidance. This ebook guide is obviously not a "do it yourself" manual for Florida divorce. However, it hopefully has given you some new, cool ways to think about your divorce-related problems (and potential solutions).

The reason I do what I do – and why my team does what it does – is to help women like you regain confidence, poise, and clarity after divorce. To that end, appreciate that we are here for you! If you need a point of law explained, or a resource, or general assistance with a divorce or family law issue, please let us know.

If you've been reading this book, and you haven't yet retained a Florida divorce attorney, please get in touch with the Quick Law Group right away to set up a consultation at **904-241-0012**.

Call The Quick Law Group at 904-241-0012 for a consultation about your Florida divorce, or to learn more please visit TheQuickLawGroup.com.

DISCLAIMER for *Women's Guide to Divorce in Florida*

THE QUICK LAW GROUP IS PROVIDING "Women's Guide to Divorce in Florida" (HEREAFTER REFERRED TO AS "BOOK") AND ITS CONTENTS ON AN "AS IS" BASIS AND MAKES NO REPRESENTATIONS OR WARRANTIES OF ANY KIND WITH RESPECT TO THIS BOOK OR ITS CONTENTS. THE QUICK LAW GROUP DISCLAIMS ALL SUCH REPRESENTATIONS AND WARRANTIES, INCLUDING FOR EXAMPLE WARRANTIES OF MERCHANTABILITY AND FITNESS FOR A PARTICULAR PURPOSE. IN ADDITION, THE QUICK LAW GROUP DOES NOT REPRESENT OR WARRANT THAT THE INFORMATION ACCESSIBLE VIA THIS BOOK IS ACCURATE, COMPLETE OR CURRENT.

Except as specifically stated in this book, neither The Quick Law Group nor any authors, contributors, or other representatives will be liable for damages arising out of or in connection with the use of this book. This is a comprehensive limitation of liability that applies to all damages of any kind, including (without limitation) compensatory; direct, indirect or consequential damages; loss of data, income or profit; loss of or damage to property and claims of third parties.

This book provides content related to topics about health. As such, use of this book implies your acceptance of the terms described herein.

You understand that this book is not intended as a substitution for a consultation with a Florida attorney.

You understand that there are risks associated with engaging in any activity described in this book. Any action you take implies that you assume all risks, known and unknown, inherent to lifestyle changes, including nutrition, exercise and any other physical activities and/or injuries which may result from the actions you take.

You hereby release The Quick Law Group and the publisher from any liability related to this book to the fullest extent permitted by law. This includes any damages, costs, or losses of any nature arising from the use of this book and the information provided by this book, including direct, consequential, special, punitive, or incidental damages, even if The Quick Law Group has been advised of the possibility of such damages.

Call The Quick Law Group at 904-241-0012 for a consultation about your Florida divorce, or to learn more please visit **TheQuickLawGroup.com**.

www.ingramcontent.com/pod-product-compliance
Lightning Source LLC
Chambersburg PA
CBHW070719180526
45167CB00004B/1543